SMOKE
FROM THIS
ALTAR

Bantam Books by Louis L'Amour
Ask your bookseller for the books you have missed.

NOVELS
Bendigo Shafter
Borden Chantry
Brionne
The Broken Gun
The Burning Hills
The Californios
Callaghen
Catlow
Chancy
The Cherokee Trail
Comstock Lode
Conagher
Crossfire Trail
Dark Canyon
Down the Long Hills
The Empty Land
Fair Blows the Wind
Fallon
The Ferguson Rifle
The First Fast Draw
Flint
Guns of the Timberlands
Hanging Woman Creek
The Haunted Mesa
Heller with a Gun
The High Graders
High Lonesome
Hondo
How the West Was Won
The Iron Marshal
The Key-lock Man
Kid Rodelo
Kilkenny
Killoe
Kilrone
Kiowa Trail
Last of the Breed
Last Stand at Papago
   Wells
The Lonesome Gods
The Man Called Noon
The Man From
   Skibbereen

The Man From the
   Broken Hills
Matagorda
Milo Talon
The Mountain Valley War
North to the Rails
Over on the Dry Side
Passin' Through
The Proving Trail
The Quick and the Dead
Radigan
Reilly's Luck
The Rider of Lost Creek
Rivers West
The Shadow Riders
Shalako
Showdown at Yellow
   Butte
Silver Canyon
Sitka
Son of a Wanted Man
Taggart
The Tall Stranger
To Tame a Land
Tucker
Under the Sweetwater
   Rim
Utah Blaine
The Walking Drum
Westward the Tide
Where the Long Grass
   Blows

SHORT STORY
   COLLECTIONS
Bowdrie
Bowdrie's Law
Buckskin Run
Dutchman's Flat
The Hills of Homicide
Law of the Desert Born
Long Ride Home
Lonigan
Night Over the Solomons

The Outlaws of Mesquite
The Rider of the Ruby
   Hills
Riding for the Brand
The Strong Shall Live
The Trail to Crazy Man
War Party
West From Singapore
Yondering

SACKETT TITLES
Sackett's Land
To the Far Blue
   Mountains
The Warrior's Path
Jubal Sackett
Ride the River
The Daybreakers
Sackett
Lando
Mojave Crossing
Mustang Man
The Lonely Men
Galloway
Treasure Mountain
Lonely on the Mountain
Ride the Dark Trail
The Sackett Brand
The Sky-Liners

NONFICTION
Education of a Wandering
   Man
Frontier
The Sackett Companion
   A Personal Guide to
   the Sackett Novels
A Trail of Memories
   The Quotations of
   Louis L'Amour,
   compiled by
   Angelique L'Amour

POETRY
Smoke from This Altar

LOUIS L'AMOUR

SMOKE FROM THIS ALTAR

BANTAM BOOKS

NEW YORK • TORONTO • LONDON

SYDNEY • AUCKLAND

Many of these poems previously appeared in Shards, Versecraft, Kaleidograph, Tanager, Prairie Winds, The Bard, Expression, Arrow, Southernesque, Embryo, and Don't Worry. Some were reprinted in North Dakota Singing, the Oklahoma Poetry Society Anthology, and Moon In The Steeple. To the editors of these publications I wish to extend grateful acknowledgment.

SMOKE FROM THIS ALTAR

A Bantam Book / December 1990

Library of Congress Cataloging-in-Publication Data

L'Amour, Louis, 1908–1988
   Smoke from this altar / Louis L'Amour.
     p.   cm.
   ISBN 0-553-07349-4
   I. Title.
PS3523.A446S6   1990
811'.52—dc20
                                     90-45677
                                     CIP

Published simultaneously in the United States and Canada

PRINTED IN THE UNITED STATES OF AMERICA

RRDH   0 9 8 7 6 5 4 3 2 1

To Singapore Charlie,
. . . . . . who couldn't read

BIOGRAPHICAL NOTE

From The Original Edition

Louis L'Amour, adventurer, soldier of fortune, and writer, was born in Jamestown, North Dakota, on the 22nd of March, 1908. Fifteen years later he began the wanderings that were to lead him into many of the strange and remote quarters of the globe. Drifting from port to port, and from country to country, he was variously occupied as seaman, miner, lumberjack, deep-sea diver, prizefighter, side-show barker, actor, reporter, and editor.

It was during those years that the material for these poems accumulated, as the titles of many of them will indicate. They were years that found him wandering in Japan, China, Borneo, Java, Sumatra, New Guinea, the Straits Settlements, India, Arabia, Egypt, and along the coasts of South and Central America. These are the memories and intimate glimpses of an interested observer.

Mr. L'Amour's short stories, articles, and poetry, have appeared in many national magazines. His first novel is now in the hands of a publisher.

CONTENTS

INTRODUCTION by Kathy L'Amour

The first book Louis purchased for his own library was *The Standard Book of British and American Verse*. It was published in 1932 and much used and loved. It is still in our library, now in its second binding. Louis' love of poetry and the English language was so strong and important in his life that it carried him through many dangerous and lonely days. At the time, poetry was the expression of Louis' most important thoughts and feelings. It was the first manner in which he wrote about his life, his views and the places he had seen. Some of these poems got published in various newspapers and magazines, and though he made only a few dollars from these sales, they gave him the optimism to keep writing.

One of his most encouraging moments came in 1936, when he received a letter from George Riley Hall, the editor of the *Daily Free-Lance*, about his poem, "Banked Fires," which had just been published in the *Daily Oklahoman*. A section of the letter read: ". . . The poem is exquisite. . . . The craftsmanship shows the master workman. . . . The imagery is all one could ask. The treatment is skilled. The sentiment one that will appeal to millions. There is one line that is worthy of the old masters—'The arching of a dream across the years.' A gifted writer might produce a whole volume and not write a line like that."

Louis returned to the United States in the late nineteen

thirties, after years at sea. He moved in with his parents on a small farm near Choctaw, Oklahoma, that Parker, his brother, had bought for them a few years before. He was thirty years old, and knew that if he was ever going to make something of himself as a writer he had better get started. He began writing short story after short story but they almost always were rejected. I think that he must have felt very tempted to leave again, to go back to the kind of life he had lived before he settled down and forced himself to think about his future. You can feel that wanderlust calling to him in his poems, "I'm a Stranger Here," "Words From a Wanderer," and "I Shall Go Back." He even wrote about putting his old life behind him and facing his future in "Let Me Forget," the poem that he used to close the *Yondering* collection.

Earlier, he had taken a few stabs at poetry. In the beginning he didn't even know about rhyme and meter. A friend who read some of his attempts in the late twenties told him that "it didn't scan." He had no idea what she was talking about, but being Louis, back to the library he went to read and reread Wordsworth, Browning, Tennyson, Frost, and Service, to discover just what it was that made a great poem.

During his travels he would occasionally compose poems, and it always seemed remarkable to me that he could both create and then remember them without writing them down; it seemed as if he could never forget a line or even a word. Louis explained that before the development of writing, poetry was one of the tricks ancient people used to remember stories. The rhyme and meter of each line would help you to remember the next. Because of this, poems that told a story, like those of Robert Service, were very popular with the hobos and sailors of his day. They were men with few possessions, some even illiterate, and so they were, in a way, like those ancient people who carried their literature in their heads.

One night in a ship's foc'stle, Louis had been trying to work out a particularly romantic poem when several of the other seamen began to tease him about only being able to write "love-stuff." After several hours of work he presented them with "My Three Friends," proving that he indeed had other talents.

When we first began dating, Louis gave me a copy of *Smoke From This Altar,* and through it I began to learn a little about the man who would become my husband and the father of our children. Many of the poems are about what he saw and thought and felt while he was in China and the South Pacific; others are about places he visited that we went back to together. We drove out to Secret Pass, the subject of a poem in this book, just after we got married. If I remember correctly, it is on the old Hardyville stage road outside of Kingman, Arizona. "Biography In Stone" was written about an outcropping of rock that Louis thought looked slightly like a man; he had become fascinated by it when he was a young man working at the Katherine Mine in the same area. "Enchanted Mesa" was written sixty years ago about what he saw when he first came through the area just west of where we now have our ranch.

Because he was having little luck with his other writing, Louis decided that he would collect the best of his poetry into a book. He hoped that publishing it would bring him some attention and prestige. A small Oklahoma City publishing company finally agreed to release *Smoke From This Altar* in 1939. Although not very many copies were sold, the book was well reviewed. Kenneth Kaufman, editor of the book page for the *Daily Oklahoman*, wrote, "What struck me first was his delight in and love for words; and what struck me next was his industry. He has that infinite capacity for taking pains, which Carlyle, I believe it was, gave as a definition of genius. And he has the ability to take punishment which only a trained fighter (which he is, along with all his other accomplishments) could stand. By which I mean to imply that he will be heard from in a big way one of these days. . . . For he has the three things which it takes to make a writer: a love for words, industry, and something to say."

Because of *Smoke From This Altar*, Louis was able to move into a different phase as a writer. He began to receive requests to speak, read his poetry, and autograph. He had published his first book, and it served to move his career along. About the same time a few of his short stories sold and he was on his way as a writer of note.

I've decided to add a few poems that weren't in the original *Smoke From This Altar*. Some are humorous, some light verse, and some serious and thoughtful. I hope you enjoy them.

SMOKE
FROM THIS
ALTAR

OUT OF THE OCEAN DEPTHS
SOUNDLESSLY MOVING

Out of the ocean depths
    soundlessly moving—
Up from the violet
    unblossoming sea;
Out of the vastness
    that strangely disturbing,
Troubles my heart
    with mute colloquy;

Out of the distance
    that holds me enchanted,
Up from the green,
    shifting violence below—
A voice from the twilight,
    the beauty, the stillness,
A voice that comes calling
    and calling to go.

Out of the purple
    along the horizon,
Up from the endless
    unchallenged beyond—
A call that comes whispering,
    softly, enduring—

Of ways to go wandering,
   seas so alluring.

Out of the ocean depths
   soundlessly moving—
Up from my memories
   disturbing and deep;
A spirit that urges me
   restlessly onward,
A dreaming that haunts me
   awake and asleep.

SMOKE FROM THIS ALTAR

Nothing has life more beautiful than ships
   Nothing with half their white-winged majesty,
   Nothing the fancy captures, roving free,
Can equal cloud-crowned masts or prow that dips
Into the waves . . . no sight can this eclipse . . .
   For here has man put wings across the sea,
   Harnessed the winds to labor, daringly,
Challenged the gods with brine upon his lips.

Give us this beauty that will conquer power,
   Give us this strength that will defy the fates . . .
The creak of wind-whipped rigging for an hour
   And splendor of the sails . . . this expiates;
Give us this glory . . . we must not forget,
   That man is noble, too, in silhouette.

INTERLUDE: HONGKONG HARBOR

The harbor lights are shining from the quay
   Like golden daggers in the heart of night;
   I stand below the lonely anchor light
And watch the sleeping city down the bay;
The world about is faint and far away—
   A thing of understanding more than sight,
   And with the dawn, like some enchanted rite,
It rises from the mist to meet the day.

The shades of night have set their sombre sail
   And fled before the crimson scythe of dawn;
The stars go out, like candles in a gale
   And leave a scene some artist might have drawn,
Of ships aflame and spires in golden mail
   That hesitates a moment and is gone.

WORDS FROM A WANDERER

I do not know your wooded slopes and streams
    But as the passing stranger knows the way
    The nets of dusk have trapped the ending day,
When webs of shadow snare the filtered gleams;
I only know how dim the pathway seems
    And how the dust from many roads of gray,
    Has sunk into my heart and made me pay
With tears and loneliness for these few dreams.

I do not know the way the hearth-light burns
    Nor how the kiss of childish lips may feel,
I only know the way the mad sea churns
    And how the blowing spray, like bits of steel,
Can tear like savage teeth, and rip from me,
    These last reluctant hopes, and leave me free.

TO CLEONE: IN BUDAPEST

You were so sure your warmth and love would hold
And you did not think of the trade wind's whine,
Nor could you know the lands I'd known of old,
Or that the paths you knew were never mine.

You did not guess the curse of common things,
Or that the bonds of love could ever chafe;
You thought the eagle's firmly pinioned wings
Were bound so very close that love was safe;

And then one night when stars were soft and clear,
Like harbor lights in some strange port of call—
I dropped my off-shore lines and harbor gear,
And sailed away to sea and left it all.

I'M A STRANGER HERE

If I, between two suns, should go away,
   No voice would lift to ask another why,
   No word would question my retreat, nor sigh,
Nor wonder why I'd chosen not to stay;
For I'm a stranger here, of other clay;
   A guest within this house, a passerby—
   A roving life whose theme has been "Goodbye"
A shadow on the road, a thing astray.

What dim ancestral heritage is mine
   That now awakens in my blood regret?
What destiny is this, what strange design,
   That I must seek a haunting silhouette
In unremembered lands my dreams divine,
   But cannot quite recall nor quite forget?

WITHOUT THIS LAND

These tawny hills cannot be mine, for here
Am I a stranger too, an alien thing
Swept up by some uncertain tide, or blown
By casual winds; these stubbled fields that lie
So impotent beneath the autumn sun
Gathering strength before the quickening urge
Of spring will swell the soil with some
New birth, and green will grow the cotton then,
And corn-lands sun themselves to life anew
Beneath familiar skies, but fields I know
The moment only, then no more, for I
Shall pass and sink no roots within this soil.
The pasture here cannot be mine to feel
Nor yet these dwarfish trees that twist above
Whining their anguish to the winter wind.
Not here am I to lean against a tree,
Feeling the furrowed bark beneath my hand
And knowing it and I were rooted deep
In this same loam; not here am I to feel
The soil is one with me, with this my flesh,
This heart, this brain; not here am I at home
Nor yet upon the sea where long slate swells
And slowly heaves and rolls and flings itself
Against the bulwarked rocks, to roll again
And yet again with long repeated blows.
Not here am I at home, for this quick flesh

Is born of many seas and many roads—
Is one with dust and wind-blown spume, and leaves
That fall and feed themselves to earth again.
These things I know but as the passerby
With many other things before, beyond—
This land, these hills, those ships and seas are all
A part of me, my flesh is of that dust,
That rain, that brine, that song is in my blood;
The dust of many roads is now my flesh,
And dust to dust returns, so this must strive
Ever returning to the roads again,
And I am rooted neither there nor here
But am a stranger to this soil, this hearth.

LIFE

I dream, and my dreams are all broken;
I love and my loving is vain . . .
I speak, and the words are all spoken,
I look and see nothing but pain.

BIOGRAPHY IN STONE

It still was dark when he paused at the desert's edge—
Above, the ridges lay like a sleeping beast
Against a sky where late stars hung like lamps
Suspended from a canopy of shade.
Standing alone, he watched the morning begin,
A bigger man than most, and marked by life
With lines of pain, with moulded power and strength.
In the east the pale bacillus of the sun
Faded the darkness with a misted glow—
The shadows, too reluctantly at bay,
Yielded before the slow advance of dawn,
And a crimson arrow hurled a flame across
The clouds to sear the sable from the sky
Except where dying darkness dripped a blood
Of shadows in the lee of shattered cliffs.

Already a massive head was taking form,
Growing from the granite into brows and nose—
A sombre etching against the dawning light;
Hands upon hips he stared upward, watching
The morning paint a blush upon the cliff,
A thousand feet of sheer, unbroken rock
Thrusting itself up boldly from the sand.
From twenty miles away it could be seen,
The highest point in all that rocky range;
Crossing the valley's floor it gripped the eye,

A monument in stone where years had left
No blemish more than did the shadows of cloud
Floating so lazily across the sun.
Slowly his sculptor's eye took in the line
Of that gigantic head, feeling its way
Across those heavy brows and where the eyes
Were soon to be. It was too great a task—
Too much for any man in one short life.
Out of that stolid stone his mind had thought
To create something grand that would remain,
A silent symbol of the strength of men,
To last through many years—a guardian
Of the sands whose tranquil brow was evidence
That here Man dreamed, and dreaming dealt with stone,
Carving the greatness and the majesty of Man
Into this timeless form to leave behind
A mute protest against futility.

Turning away, he took the mountain trail
Winding upward across the precipice,
A narrow path that was a slender thread
Suspended there between achievement and death;
A rolling rock beneath his careless foot
Might be the fitting end to such a dream,
And check with one swift plunge his carving hands.
Thinking of it, he smiled, and looked back down

The dizzy height, quite unafraid of falling.
At last he reached the top and stood alone.
Darkly, against the amber light of dawn
He watched the evanescent sun rays climb,
Then turned to sort his gear before the day
Of work began, yet pausing time to time
To deeply breath and watch an eagle soar
Above the cliff; sometimes it dropped so low
It seemed to sweep his head with slanting wing.
"Look out, old bird, you're coming close!" he said,
"But we've a lot in common—did you guess?"
Below, a rattling car disgorged three men,
Who saw his figure etched against the sky.
"He's a man, that one!" the older man remarked.
"It's all a dream, but what a splendid dream!
Ours would be a better world if more
Could dream like that. But it's too big for us."
"He's a fool, Casey. Why spend his gold like that?
I'd never do the like as long as beer
And women last. He worked too hard, then sold
His claim, and puts the money into this.
But what a job! I like it, too, but I
Don't have to pay the bills. Let's go aloft."
Silently mounting across a golden cliff,
And joining Morgan above the lofty brow
They lowered staging down the precipice

Descending to their work.
                    Day after day
Their muscles shaped the cliff, the stone took form
As though a Titan stepped from living rock;
The shoulders, hands and feet half-shaped by wind
And rain and sun before the work began.
"See, Casey," Morgan said. "It's not so hard.
I used to wonder no one saw the lines
Before I came along—it all was here.
A rounding here and there, a needed touch,
And just like that the figure takes its form.
The face alone remains, and that's the job."
"Ay, a job is right. How long did this—
This man of yours stand waiting for an eye?
How many million years will men go by
And wonder at the hand that carved this stone?"
"They'll wonder then, for all of me. My name
Is only a symbol for a certain thing,
A certain face and hands, and certain thoughts;
The face and hands will go—this job will last—
The bundled dreams and lies, the doubt and hope,
The things that make up Me, they will be gone;
My flesh and blood will turn to grass perhaps,
To feed the cows that feed the young of fools.
So why the name? I like the job itself,
It's something for a man with guts to do,

The job is big enough and grand enough, but small
At that; I used to work my claim and dream
Of this, or in the mines, a thousand feet
Below, I'd curse the heat and change my steel,
Thinking of this, and how some day I'd shape
A figure here the sun would strike each dawn—
How passing men would mark this splendid thing,
And moving on, might dream great dreams themselves."
He paused, and turned to face the old man.
"But now, my Irish friend, there's more to say.
You boys had better go—I'm running short,
And there's an even chance you'll not be paid
If you stay on. I've liked you all, and wish
There were some other way, but after all
It's up to me, I'll finish here alone."

The days crept by like cogs upon a wheel
Leaving their mark upon that brooding face,
Where single-jack and chisel shaped each line,
Lifting the features from the stone as though
Only the form were being chipped away,
And behind that rocky mask the face had lived
Waiting in silence for the artist's hand.

McLain, an engineer from Frisco, stopped
His car and climbed the trail to watch the work,

Almost completed now. He saw the man
Descend the cliff, then turned his eyes to note
The skill with which the art had shaped the stone,
Suggesting lines like wraiths beneath the rock
As though the spirit of the mountain stirred,
Awakening at last to life and strength.
"Morgan! I might have known you were the one.
But even you . . . why, Man, I've never seen such work!
Does it have a name? Is it Hercules or Thor?"
He looked again upon that sombre face,
Bathed now in sunset rays, aloft, alone;
There was grandeur there, and solitude and strength,
And some nobility not quite beyond
The grasp of men, some beauty there, and calm.
But nothing there of gods, but only men—
And sympathy no god could understand.
"No thunder-hurling god could have a face
Like that," Morgan replied. "He's just a man,
I would not have him more. A man and a dream,
For all the things that man has built are dreams;
A man conceives, a man creates, he builds
And then destroys that he may build again.
I think that it would be a splendid thing
If men were big enough, like that—" he waved
A hand up toward the face; compassionate,
All-seeing strength revealed in every line.

"They could forget their little jealousies,
Their petty hates and greeds, the futile lines
They draw of race and creed—they could be free.
For Man is less than nothing in himself—
His works reveal him best; there's grandeur there,
And beauty, power, and the glory of his dreams.
In a thousand lands a thousand altars lift
Their incense to the sky—to the gods, perhaps?
More likely to Man's better self, his dreams,
Ideals and hopes. But I've a job to do,
And that's enough."
                    Low-flying dusk caressed
The hills, the fingered pinnacles grew tall,
And in the canyons, narrow-mouthed, the dark
Flowered against the walls, and gaunt white fangs
Of cacti gnawed the sky. High overhead
The stone man faced the night, a resting hand
Upon a granite knob. A motor whined
Across the valley floor, a distant sound
Returning McLain to work and tomorrow.
And Morgan waited the sound away, then took
The downward path to the 'dobe beside the walls.
He hesitated, staring down the road
Toward Coyote Pass and the people and cities beyond.
"I wonder if they'll ever come this way?
And mass along these desert floors, to build

Their homes of this red rock? Or will they pass
And leave the desert here alone with me?
I may be here. That rocky shape contains
Too much of me to leave, too much of cold
And hunger's written there in that still face,
Too much of loneliness and suffering, too.
I wanted a job that was big enough for a man—
Being mid-wife to a mountain's big enough.
I've hammered there, and carved until I know
Each curve and crack, each notch upon the stone.
The biography of man is written there
In every line of that great granite face,
The biography of man, and all his dreams.
Someday I'll shake the dust from off my shoes
And leave it all behind, the whole damned thing."

A wind from down the ranges touched the sand
And whispered there among the cactus spines,
His memory stirred, and he recalled the road,
But shrugged and turned away to take the path.
In the still night desert air a coyote called,
And a burro bell in the moonlight sounded clear.
Dark silence filled the hollow of the hills—
Somewhere a pebble rattled down the rocks
And the stone man stared into the years before
Where centuries gathered their dust and confusion.

AN EMBER IN THE DARK

Faintly, along the shadowed shores of night
I saw a wilderness of stars that flamed
And fluttered as they climbed or sank, and shamed
The crouching dark with shyly twinkling light;
I saw them there, odd fragments quaintly bright,
And wondered at their presence there unclaimed,
Then thought, perhaps, that they were dreams unnamed,
That faded slow, like hope's arrested flight.

Or vanished suddenly, like futile fears—
And some were old and worn like precious things
That youth preserves against encroaching years—
Some disappeared like songs that no man sings,
   But one remained—an ember in the dark—
   I crouched alone, and blew upon the spark.

NOCTURNE

The stars unveil
As clouds regale
   Themselves with flight,
The moon, a moth
Whom loves betroth
   To summer night.

The trees a fringe
That darkly cringe
   Along the sky;
And I, alone,
Regret I've known
   That love can die.

The hours sound deep,
I cannot sleep
   For love is gone;
No stars remain
To mourn my pain
   Or greet the dawn.

WINGS OVER WAVES

They lightly tread on dancing feet
  With elfin steps to lilting beat
Upon the level sand;
  Where wind and wave contrive to meet
They race along, then stop, and go
To dodge the sea's returning flow—
They sail about on wings of snow
  Above the silent strand.

Then stepping quickly, lightly trace
  Queer hieroglyphs upon the face
Of dampened sand with fairy grace
  Before the changing sea;
Their fingered feet in signs grotesque
Step out their weaving arabesque
Or pose in manner picturesque
  With sombre gravity.

They balance through a queer quadrille
  And weave strange patterns with their skill
Or call in voices loud and shrill
  Above the ocean's roar;
They light on rocks to primp and preen
And flirt in manner quite serene
Or float above the ocean's green
  Along the lonely shore.

A HANDFUL OF STARS

Give me, O Night, a blessing
  Of peace, and a handful of stars—
Give me, O Dawn, a beginning,
  New life, and a healing of scars;
Give me, O Day, a freshening
  Of spirit, and warmth in the sun—
Give me, O Earth, of thy bounty,
  Strength for the task I've begun.

Leave me, O Night, of your stillness
  A calm for my inward soul—
Leave me a breath of your darkness
  To cool me, and keep me whole;
Leave me the wind in the willows
  The roll of the surf and the sea—
Leave me, Beloved, my memories
  Of dreams you have given to me.

WINTER

Bare trees standing stark
Against the sky, lifting
Thin, imploring arms
To the cold gray clouds.

SECRET PASS

Those hills remember me, for I alone
  Sought out their solitudes and silent ways;
  The harsh, forbidding cliffs and canyon maze
Recall each step I took, each path I've known;
No trees are there, but barren butte and cone,
  And empty aisles where long, lost shadows graze—
  Or wind-worn monuments that marked my days
With all the voiceless eloquence of stone.

If only I possessed their fortitude,
  Their sombre freedom from this searing pain!
If only I could lose in solitude,
  These hollow, useless hopes that still remain!
If only I could find my heart subdued,
  And cease its sounding on that old refrain!

BANKED FIRES

I shall remember when my days are few
   The twilight on a narrow, winding road;
   The slender silver moon that days corrode;
The star that lent its loveliness to you.
The arching of a dream across the years—
   I shall remember with the slow-winged night
   The shadow of your hair against the light
Of locust trees abloom with frosted tears.

I shall remember when my fires are low,
   The way you looked at me; the words you used;
The fragrance of your hurried breath, till lo,
   Through all the pain of love our spirits fused.
   I shall remember when my fires cease
   Your heart against my own—for that was peace.

NORTH CAPE

A hollow hand of hills that clutches dawn
Close in their impotent grasp, as fading slow,
The shadows slip away before the day
And leave the sun behind; its filtered glow
Can leave no warmth on slopes so sparsely clad,
But sickly lies among the brown blades there,
Helpless against this cold, impassive earth;
Even the stones are numb and stubborn here—
Even the dust lies flat against the road—
Even the streams to immobility
Are chilled, to frozen pathways here, no joy
Of water whispering to the stones, but stark
And sullen silence down these empty hills.
Even the wings of death avoid this place,
Avoid these barren fields, for Death itself
Must nestle to the warmth of life and youth,
And nothing dies where nothing lives. These men
Wither away and fall, but do not die;
They age, but not with years, they die but not
With death, but with the chill of things out-worn.
No youth is here, for these are born to age;
Even the summer sun is haunted here
With chilled and doubting glow, then fades away.

And what to these can mean the Renaissance,
The fire that flamed in Florence and gave birth

To Angelo, Leonardo, and their dreams?
These fires are frozen here, and numb with cold—
The unresponding hills—gray seas, gray earth,
Gray clouded skies—no warmth of blues or greens.
Even the passions here are cold and dull;
That Athens was, that Plato dreamed, that Poe
Had haunted nights with hunger from his heart,
Or Byron sang of love—what mean these things
To these? This is the land of Thor, but not
Of Aphrodite—no Pan could be conceived
Upon these sleeping slopes or in these thoughts.
For there is only strength and hard hands formed
To fierceness and to fury here . . . and cold.

TO YOU, JEANNINE

The wind's an owl
Who likes to prowl
    The night serene,
A drifting ghost
Who blows to boast
    Around you, Jeannine.

The star-lit fleece
Of clouds at peace
    With night between,
Recalls a thought
Of dreams I wrought
    For you, Jeannine.

The curtained light
Forbids the light
    To intervene,
The moon has heard
My whispered word
    To you, Jeannine.

DECADENCE

I sit alone and watch the stars die out
    Before the creeping dawn comes up the sky,
Like some old priest whose faith has turned to doubt
    When gods no longer heed his wailing cry.

The dark trees etch themselves against the dawn,
    Like memories of old that bring regret,
Or little formless fears the night has drawn
    Against the sky in sharp-lined silhouette.

The moon is fading now, the skies grow gray—
    The turning tide of life is at its ebb,
And mists along the valley float away
    Like silvery dew upon a spider's web.

This world is dying now; there is no more—
    A dawn will come more hopeless than the night,
Our rhymes are run, our hopes no longer soar,
    We bow beneath a barren beauty's blight.

The ashes of our altar fires are cold,
    And prophets wail the times they cannot mend—
Facing the future with hearts grown old
    We only know . . . a world can end.

LOVE OUT OF SEASON

The spring is gone, but left behind with me
    Untempered fever raging in my veins,
    Unkind remembrance of the April rains,
And something of its own glad gaiety;
To be in love in spring is best, you see,
    When warming earth's alive with growing pains,
    And cherry petals fill the tangled skeins
The spider spins between the fence and tree.

But summer's come, and that infernal spring
    Has left this love behind—the season's wrong,
And I should think of keeping cool, and bring
    Tranquillity, and less impassioned song
To share my bed, and yet the whole night through
    I lie awake and swear—and think of you.

AFTER TOMORROW

No more but this—no more but echoes down
The lonely hills, and breathless hush—did Man
Perhaps, in movement pass this way, and plan
Some transitory edifice or town?
And did some brain-created glory crown
This hill, imposing while the moments ran
A stately emptiness that failed to span
The years that saw his passing, saint and clown?

Where now the bubble-dreams that stabbed the sky,
The cloud-encroaching spires of steel and glass?
Where now the thunder-throated guns of death
Who breathed their anguish with a whinning cry?
The scars are healed, the ghostly streets are grass—
Man and his wonders vanished, like a breath.

YACODHAPURA

I stood within the high-arched temple doors
   Within a columned hall at close of day,
   Where once the solemn crowds had come to pray
And kneel in silence on the dusty floors;
I wandered down the roofless corridors
   Where Time's relentless hand had carved its way
   Along the wind-worn walls of stolid gray
Where nature wages endless wearing wars.

Above, beyond, the slowly setting sun
Painted the towering columns one by one,
   And lit the halls with mute tranquillity;
Some sculptured dreams in dull, time-tarnished stone
Looming long years, forgotten and alone—
   A shadowed symbol of futility.

STEPPE

Beneath a barren sky the crusted snow
    Lies cold and lifeless like a frozen sea;
    The lonely, prowling wind moans eerily
And loiters, sighing, like the voice of woe;
A land, unborn and still where weary blow
    The icy winds in cold hostility,
    While earth and sky in gray monotony
With cheerless consonance, together flow.

What bleak and impotent old world is this?
    No whistling blast, but dull, and numb, and still
    Unending miles where frigid plains deny
The throbbing urge of life, the warming kiss
    Of fire, and naught but fitful puffs of chill
    And piercing winds beneath a rheumy sky.

TO GIORDANO BRUNO

(Martyr of science, 1548–1600)

You were the best of them, Bruno, the best
By more than the flames that fired your flesh
    to dust—
The best by more than the truth you framed
    your lips
To speak. The One was All, the All was One,
And the only law the ever changing form.
What did you think as the lambent light crept up
Licking your limbs with tongue that seared
    and charred?
Did you think then, Bruno, that the flame was Change
Returning the One to All, the flesh to dust?
Your seven years were long, yet longer still
The moments when the candent light crept up
Enfolding your flesh with fervent flames to char
The hope there must have been, to stifle truth
With caustic brand, to still the voice that spoke.
Did you remember then, Bruno, that will
Was ever free? The fathers lit the fire,
And hung like ghouls along its outer edge,
But were the flames less bright because
    they blackened
The lips of truth? I wonder if the blaze
That sheathed your form with lustful heat
    turned white

Around that mighty heart? Around that brain?
The one who muttered that "The earth still moves,"
He was a wiser, if not a better man;
For aging hearts are brittle on the pyre.
You spoke too often, Friend; had you forgot
The insignificant ever dislike
To be reminded of insignificance?
You were the best of them, Bruno, the best
By more than the flames that wrought the Change
In the monads of your soul. As the flames
Engulfed in fiery foam your anguished lips,
Did you dying, wonder at those foolish ones
Who sought to stifle truth with violence?

THE WEARY ONE

I wandered along the dusty way
   seeking the dawn of another day,
     like a drifting chip on a lonely stream,
     like a breath of wind or a vagrant dream
  a forgotten soul on a weary quest
searching for home and love and rest.

I wandered along the dusty way
   and found my idols with feet of clay,
     my letters were ashes, my castles dust—
     the sword I wielded eaten by rust,
  my dreams were shattered—a heavy load
is all that is left on a winding road.

HILDEBRAND

He walked away at dusk, and it was long
Before we met again; in Singapore
One night on Malay Street (a corridor
Of darkness cleft with light) I heard a song—
Among ten thousand I could not be wrong—
A voice like booming seas along the shore
Singing an old, old tune once sung before
The mast on tea ships bound for old Hongkong.

He waved to me—a bottle and a girl—
I saw him not again, but once I heard
A seaman tell of storms along the strand,
Of great, wet rocks where foaming combers curl,
And of a seaman, blonde and tall, and stirred
By fires of fury—that was Hildebrand.

ENCHANTED MESAS

Weary at last with way-worn wandering
   I paused to rest in solemn solitude,
Watching the sinking sun, and pondering
   Upon the desert's melancholy mood;
The falling dark had left the day subdued,
   And crowned the sullen hills with fading light;
Huge boulders loomed, a black and battered brood,
   Like dark, unholy spectres in the night,
And gathered clans of wind went moaning in their
   flight.

Along the burnt-out ridges wind-swept rocks
   Heaved granite backs against the evening sky,
A brutal, barren land whose silence mocks
   Man's empty efforts to identify
His works with these exhausted hills, that lie
   Like some abandoned world left desolate,
Whose stark remains are all that signify
   Some half-completed effort to create
From fires that fused these hills and left them
   devastate.

These blasted rocks, so lifeless, numb, and still—
   A land of mighty cliffs that stand aghast
Upon the desert's brink, without the will
   To face the yucca's mute battalions, massed

Like nightmare creatures from the ages past
    Returned to conquer fiefs they knew of old;
These crumbling walls, and rambling ramparts vast,
    And tumbled stones from nature's shattered mold—
Their solitude is mine, and all their moonlit gold.

Like clinkers from an ash-heap of the gods—
    Or toys of Titans, torn and tossed away;
Grim monuments to war against the odds
    Of storm and rain, or winds that wildly play
Across the cacti-studded sands to flay
    With violence, and seek to overwhelm
These rocky spires that neither bend nor sway;
    Time has no meaning here—Space holds the helm,
And years, like clouds pass by, while silence rules the
    realm.

The canyons weave their winding arabesque
    While cliffs like frozen thunder stand aside
And weather-molded stones, in shapes grotesque
    Lean lonesomely above the desert's tide;
These hills are mine . . . their wasted flanks confide,
    Their ghostly fingered dawns reach out for me,
For we are kin, and time shall not divide
    My heart from this, our voiceless colloquy
But let us rest alone for all eternity.

MY THREE FRIENDS

I have three friends, three faithful friends,
More faithful could not be—
And every night, by the dim firelight,
They come to sit with me.

The first of these is tall and thin
With hollow cheeks, and a toothless grin;
A ghastly stare, and scraggly hair,
And an ugly lump for a chin.

The second of these is short and fat
With beady eyes, like a starving rat—
He was soaked in sin to his oily skin,
And verminous, at that.

The crouching one is of ape-like plan,
Formed like a beast that resembled man:
A freakish thing, with arms a-swing,
And he was the third of that gruesome clan.

The first I stabbed with a Chinese knife,
And left on the white beach sand,
With his ghastly stare, and blood-soaked hair,
And an out-flung, claw-like hand;

The fat one stole a crumbling crust,
That he wolfed in his swineish way—
So I left him there, with eyes a-glare,

And his head cut off half-way.

We fought to kill, the brute and I,
That the one that lived might eat,
So I killed him too, and made a stew,
And dined on human meat.

And so these three come to visit me,
When without the night winds howl—
The one with the leer, the one with a sneer,
And one with a brutish scowl;

Their lips are dumb, but the three dead come
And crouch by the hollow grate—
The man that I stabbed, the man that I cut,
And the gruesome thing that I ate.

Their lips are sealed, with blood congealed,
But they will not let me be,
And so they haunt, grim, ghastly, and gaunt,
Till death shall set me free.

I have three friends, three faithful friends,
More faithful could not be—
And every night, by the dim firelight,
They come to sit with me.

IN AN OLD TEMPLE

Into that stillness I could never thrust
A lance of sound so harsh as human word,
To stir the sleeping echoes from the dust
That now are lying empty and unheard;

I could but whisper softly to the ghosts
And linger there a moment as in prayer,
Adding another to the voiceless hosts
Unnumbered ages have abandoned there.

THE SEA, OFF VANUA LEVU

There is a beauty in this beyond believing,
　A strength that is stronger than the hands of men,
There is a glory in this that is greater than grieving
　That brings a stillness to my heart again;

There is a power in this beyond longing or laughter,
　A grandeur unmeasured by cloud or sky—
There is a sounding here, and an echo after—
　A sounding of surf and a sea-gull's cry;

There is an ending here, for the time, of emotion
　Of sorrow and sadness, of envy and fear;
All these are forgotten beside the wide ocean,
　That gray rolling splendor, cold and austere.

IF THERE IS BEAUTY

If there is any beauty after this
    Or any quiet joy, or imagery
    Of happiness that we may share, then we
Must never hesitate, nor be remiss;
If in the after years the deep abyss
    Of sorrow draws you close, and mournfully
    The old dreams die, then you must turn to me
And to this love that needs no emphasis.

If, when tomorrow comes, the things you knew
    No longer are, but like an empty town
    Whose windows catch the fading sunset flame,
Your eyes reflect your loneliness, and you
    Watch one by one the swifter years go down—
    Then turn to me, for I shall be the same.

SHIP ACROSS THE SKY

White wings across the morning,
   Dark sails against the moon,
Scudding along in the spindrift
   While the trade-winds croon;

Dark hull against the blue,
   White spars across the sky—
Like a song from out of the distance
   And clear as a sea-gull's cry;

Hull down against the horizon
   And royals across the gray,
I saw it fade into the distance
   Sailing my dreams away.

McVEY

It did not matter who or what he was
Before he came to these sun-spattered hills,
Or why he chose that wind-tormented ridge
The scene of his grim struggle with the soil;
He seemed to love it there, the sky so near
It almost touched the gnarled and twisted trees.
And often when the rain in frenzy beat
Against the staring windows and the roof,
Flooding the planted fields to leave them bare,
And mark another year of fruitless toil,
We'd see him out beneath the lowering sky
Undaunted by the storm, while lightning leaped
From pinnacle to pinnacle of cloud.
While thunder rolled and rumbled off away
Sulking and sullen like a baffled hound,
To lose itself in distance down the hills
Like the whimper of far-off trumpets, or waves
Growling among the boulders worn and old.
On sunny days he'd watch the racing clouds
Go drifting down the sky like scattered foam—
"Like ships," he'd say, "Like sailing ships at sea,
Bound outward for some port they cannot guess."

I CAME TO CREATE

I came to create on a larger scale—
To shape a universe of stars and suns,
To chart the comet's course, and map the runs
Of hurtling meteors down the midnight trail;
I came to carve out mountain-tops, to flail
Sun-burnished clouds to splendid shapes; I came
To write across the sky in words of flame
A stronger, sweeter song, a grander tale.

I came to walk with gods and found them men
So blind with greed they had not paused to see
How hunger walked with hopelessness again—
I came to create and remain to plea
For those without the words to speak, for all
The disinherited—is this so small?

LINES TO A SEASON

How quietly the year has passed away
Into that nothingness from whence it came,
And now the slowly drifting days are gray
Like powdered ashes near a dying flame;
The maple trees bewail their fallen crown
And autumn trails away like smoke at dawn—
The grass has faded to a dusty brown,
And I am lonely for a summer gone.

Each sunset tinted leaf is like a day
Blown from the tree of unrelenting years,
Leaves fall, and flowers die, lives float away,
And we are bitter now, with unshed tears.
A dying sun is setting through the gray—
How quietly the year has passed away!

I SHALL GO BACK

I shall go back—I cannot longer stay—
   The dark gods grumble in the storm tonight,
   The low winds moan, and out beyond the light
A dark sea rolls and mumbles in the bay;
I shall go back—I've been too long away
   From dim sea dawns and combers crested white,
   From ashen brows of cloud, from sound and sight
Of all the things I knew but yesterday.

Out there the hollow-hearted moon will glow
   Upon the gray, mist-haunted seas where men
   Have left no scars of wars, no beaten track;
No blaring streets, but green sea gods below—
   No ordered ways, but fog and storm again,
   And time to work and dream—I shall go back.

NEWLY
COLLECTED
POEMS

I HAVEN'T READ
GONE WITH THE WIND

I have read Shakespeare, Shelley, and Poe
    What profit is in these?
I sit alone wherever I go
    And strive to look at ease.
I crouch alone beside the wall
    To avoid their eager look—
But no matter how I stall
    They'll ask about that book.

I cannot check my sheepish blush,
    My color comes and goes,
I redden to my finger-tips
    And sometimes to my nose.
But they will leer and sneer at me—
    Their eyes triumphant shine,
Tho for every book they've read
    I've read forty-nine.

I wish I had their awful cheek—
    I'd let them have their fling
Then stories I'd tell of Boccaccio
    Not quite the proper thing;
Of Homer and Horace and Catullus
    Hudson and Halleck and Hoffenstein—

For every single book they've read
    I've read forty-nine.

No other title do they know,
    The refrain is scarcely new—
Tho the chances are their knowledge
    Came from a book review;
They ask me if I've read it—
    I humbly whisper "No"
(Thank God, again I've said it!)
    They clap their hands and glow.

I've read John Donne—I like to drift
    Thru Plato, Plutarch, and Euripides;
I know Spinoza—I've read Dean Swift,
    And Stendhal, or Sterne, or Maimonidies.
I've read Wycherley, and read Sam Pepys
    Not quite so funny, but subtler—
In spite of all that I'm down in the deeps
    I know nothing about Rhett Butler!

I'm familiar with Falstaff, Dido, and Puck
    But no one gives me a tumble—
I've done my reading—I'll have no truck
    With the thousands who chortle and rumble,
And talk about Butler and Scarlett O'Hare.

Did she right? Did she wrong? they gasp and exclaim—
If she'd morals or not, I don't seem to care
  But I'm plucking the coverlet over that name.

I'm almost a social outcast now
  For no matter where I go,
They crowd around and ask me
  Be it concert, party, show—
I hesitate as in a dream
  One would almost think I'd sinned
But if another asks me, I will scream
  NO! I haven't read *Gone With The Wind!*

IN PROTEST

Do not tell me—let me wonder
Why the populace must blunder
      Over my name?
I have waded dumbled through
Names as bad as Ruth Suckow,
And if mine's quite in a Frenchy way,
What about Bill Rose Benet?
I have bowed with proud head humbled
When over Bjorkman I have mumbled,
Or when I failed to end with "o"
The name of Dion Boucicault—
      To my shame;
But whenever I speak of Heinrich Heine
His name is rhymed with Carolina;
There still are names too tough for me,
But I ring the Belloc with Hilaire;
I've listened to recondite rabble
Who put the "T" in Tietjens, and put the "cab"
      in Cabell,
But soon the guys will be in armor
Who persist in saying "Larmour"
For I am hot upon the spoor
Of all who fail to say L'Amour
      Which is my name.

QUESTION

Here's to the lands untraveled
  And the roads I've never known,
To the high, lost lakes in the mountains
  The islands that linger alone;
Here's to the hands I've never held,
  And the lips I've never kissed—
To all the things I might have done,
  And all the things I've missed.
Here's to the eyes that look into mine,
  To the urge that's burning bright;
For my pulse beats strong and my heart
      is warm,
And . . . *what are you doing tonight?*

A WAIL FROM A PULPETEER

If I could end this servitude
To need for coin, so gross and lewd,
I'd face the world with fortitude
    No doubt.

If I had four and twenty blonds
A diamond and a stack of bonds,
Some caviar, and beer in ponds
    I'd flout

Inferior scum who write for cash
Neglect their "art" and deal in trash,
And from my pen they'd feel the lash
    Of blame.

In pleasant comfort, quite content,
I'd sit secure—and scorn I'd vent
While they wrote tripe to pay the rent
    Of shame.

I'd lash those literary lice
With patronizing "good advice"
I'd wreck their pulpy paradise
    And write

Of "selling souls" and "prostitution"—
With violent words and elocution

I'd demand their bloody execution—
       The blight!

But all the phrases that I sculp
Are buried in some woody pulp
And as my weary sobs I gulp
       I try

To scratch out stories for my meat,
    And just perhaps a Sunday treat
    For Nature tells me I must eat—
       But Why?

OLD JERRY

Old Jerry was a jolly man
   Who knew the woodland ways,
And used to trap along the creek
   Through cold and wintry days;
He often told blood-thirsty tales
   Beside the roaring fire.
Although the village folk would say
   Old Jerry was a liar.

They had no sympathy for him
   Nor his hair-raisin' yarns,
But we would often come to play
   Around his ramblin' barns—
It may not be that Jerry told
   The strict, unvarnished truth
But what was that to you or me,
   Or any listening youth?

He had a scar upon his cheek—
   "A knife in Singapore;"
He had a bullet in his arm—
   "I got it in the war."
It may be that his yarns were true
   It may be that he lied.
I only know that we were sad
   When Jerry died.

PICTURE

Gray fog steals along
The waterfront and gathers
In shadowed places . . .
Old ships doze beside the dock
Dreaming lazily . . .
Damp lumber piles loom darkly
Along narrow slips . . .
Somewhere a deep-throated blast
Echoes lonesomely . . .
With up-turned collar I slouch
Away into mist.

CALL OF THE TROPICS

There's a balmy breeze a-blowing
   Somewhere out across the sea,
And it's there that I am going
   Where the tossing waves roll free.

There's a tropic moon a-shining
   Down upon the coco-palm.
And it's for that land I'm pining
   With its drowsy, sleepy calm.

There's a great white ship a-steaming
   Out across the bounding main,
And its foaming wake is gleaming
   As it takes me back again.

THE GLADIATOR

Mine is the glory of battle
Mine whose reward is to die—
Mine is the ending death-rattle
  Without the one gift of a sigh;
Mine never the glory of conquest
Mine never the fires of a hate,
Mine only the pain and the death-rest—
  A bowing to powers of Fate.

Mine is the fury of fighting
With nothing to win or defend,
Mine is the heart that's inviting
  That deathly inevitable end;
Mine is the net and the trident
Mine is the word or the spear,
Mine were the lips the sigh sent
  I, who never knew fear.

Mine is the brain knows the ending
Before the beginning has come,
Mine whose prayers are ascending
  From lips that were never so dumb;
Mine is the heart that is longing
For the distant green hills of my home,
Mine is the life will grow thronging
  Through lips that are bloody with foam.

THE PIONEER

Across these hills you roamed so long ago
    When ringed around mute hostility—
    You blazed your trail to immortality,
And learned to know the bitterness of woe;
You passed along, and yet you served to show
    The way you came to all posterity,
    And in your passing left a legacy
Of courage to the sons that were to grow.
Where once your winding, rutted wagon trail
    Had left its scars upon the yielding plain—
    A furrowed field lies waiting in the sun.
And grazing cattle wander down the vale
    As slowly walking homeward through the lane
    They signify the peace your courage won.

TRANQUILLITY

I wander down along the oak-clad hills
   Where twilight lives beneath the tranquil trees,
   Along dim aisles untouched by passing breeze,
Where perfume that the violet distills
Becomes the essence of the shade, and fills
   With fragrance all the gloomy corridor—
I walk along the shadowed forest floor
And think of things that solitude instills.
No sound disturbs the fading afternoon
   As mellow dreams come drifting down the years,
   Remembered thoughts, a half-forgotten tune—
An endless chain of hopes, and smiles, and tears;
   So turning from almost forgotten ills,
   I wander back along the oak-clad hills.

TWILIGHT

These are the restful hours
   After the day has gone,
Before the buds of flowers
   Have changed to the blooms of dawn;
After the sun in setting
   Has brought the twilight calm
When man can rest, forgetting,
   Tranquil as a psalm.

FOREST PEOPLE

I read their story in the sand,
    Another in the snow,
They write it with their tiny feet
    As they come and go;

Here one stopped to eat awhile,
    There one paused in fear—
This was a sparrow's landing field
    With marks of his running gear;

Their joys and woes and tragedies
    Are written clear and bold.
Their swift, minute biographies
    The tracks they leave unfold.

WINTER WINDS

Now coldly blow the wintry
    winds
    Across the fields, and whining,
Sing through the trees like
    violins
    Some ghostly tune designing;
And low, gray skies above the
    hills
    Where stormy clouds are
    racing,
Are warning of the wind that
    chills
    Through branches interlacing.

Far down the avenue of trees
    It dashes sadly moaning,
Along the stream where waters
    freeze
    A plaintive song intoning;
It whines and whirls among
    the leaves
    To send them madly sailing,
Then swings around beneath
    the eaves
    The distant spring bewailing.

LET IT SNOW

Snow in the sky,
    Earth turning white—
A tree like a ghost
    In the gathering night;
Low clouds above,
    White world below—
Barn roofs and houses
    Covered with snow.

Deep in his burrow
    The 'possum is huddled,
Far in the bushes
    Snowbirds are cuddled,
The creek in the morning
    Coldly will gleam,
But I've got a fire,
    A book and a dream.

THEN CAME SPRING

The night before
　　The sunset clear
Betokened that
　　The spring was near.
When dusk came down
　　The wild geese flew,
And all night long
　　A soft wind blew;
When morning came
　　We heard bees hum,
And then we knew
　　That spring had come.

RAIN

Wind on the roof—
  Clouds in the sky,
Close by the fire
  Contented and dry;
Sitting and dreaming
  Of journeys afar,
Under the sun
  Or under a star.

Loafing alone
  And watching the rain
Beating itself
  On the window-pane
Dreaming all night
  Of sun coming soon
And listening to rain
  Singing of June.

MUTATION

A fog is on the lowlands
  In drifting, ghostly wraiths,
The tops of trees like islands
  Or spires of vanished faiths;
There's silence on the river
  Like that of brooding death
Where blades of swamp-grass shiver
  In the slightest stealing breath.

There's something in the morning.
  A hint of changing days—
There's freshness all adorning
  Along the woodland ways;
The pastel shades of May-time
  Will come and disappear
Between the dawn and day-time
  And summer will be here.

TO ONE WITHOUT FAITH

What shall I say of you in future years,
When at the bar of judgment memory stands?
What of the hope I built on shifting sands
Of love too weak to bear your faithless fears?
What shall I say of youth and bitter tears,
Of words that struck my brain like burning brands?
What shall I say of cold remorseless hands
That ground my lover's hopes like meshing gears?

Where once my heart held naught but love for you
And dreams of days we spent in ecstasy,
Or vagrant thoughts of vanished hours we knew
There now are ashes of your loyalty;
What shall I say when asked if you were true,
When faced with facts of your inconstancy?

ROSE OF MEMORY

I turned the leaves of an ancient book
    A book that was faded and worn—
And there 'tween the leaves I found a rose,
    A tiny rose, and a thorn.

Where are the lips that kissed that rose
    And the hands so soft and white,
That gave to me that rose of love,
    The love we pledged that night?

Long since those days have passed away,
    And we have drifted apart,
The blood-red rose has faded now—
    But the thorn rests deep in my heart.

LET ME FORGET

Let me forget the dark seas rolling,
The taste of wind, the lure and lift
Of far, blue shrouded shores;
No longer let the wild wind's singing
Build high the waves in this
My heart's own storm;
Now let me quietly work, for I have songs.

Let not my blood beat answer to the sea
The beaches lie alone, so let them lie;
Let me forget the gray banked distant hills,
The echoing emptiness of ancient towns;
No longer let the brown leaves falling
Move me to wander . . . I have songs to sing.

ABOUT LOUIS L'AMOUR

"I think of myself in the oral tradition—as a troubadour, a village taleteller, the man in the shadows of the campfire. That's the way I'd like to be remembered—as a storyteller. A good storyteller."

It is doubtful that any author could be as at home in the world recreated in his novels as Louis L'Amour. Not only could he physically fill the boots of the rugged characters he wrote about, but he literally "walked the land my characters walk." His personal experiences as well as his lifelong devotion to historical research combined to give Louis L'Amour the unique knowledge and understanding of people, events, and the challenge of the American frontier that became the hallmarks of his popularity.

Of French-Irish descent, Louis L'Amour could trace his own family in North America back to the early 1600s and follow their steady progression westward, "always on the frontier." As a boy growing up in Jamestown, North Dakota, he absorbed all he could about his family's frontier heritage, including the story of his great-grandfather who was scalped by Sioux warriors.

Spurred by an eager curiosity and desire to broaden his horizons, Louis L'Amour left home at the age of fifteen and enjoyed a wide variety of jobs including seaman, lumberjack, elephant handler, skinner of dead cattle, assessment miner, and officer on tank destroyers during World War II. During his "yondering" days he also circled the world on a freighter, sailed a dhow on the Red Sea, was shipwrecked in the West Indies and stranded in the Mojave Desert. He won fifty-one of fifty-nine fights as a professional boxer and worked as a journalist and lecturer. He was a voracious reader and collector of books. His personal library contains 17,000 volumes.

Louis L'Amour "wanted to write almost from the time I could talk." After developing a widespread following for his many frontier and adventure stories written for fiction magazines, he published his first full-length novel, *Hondo,* in the United States in 1953. Every one of his more than 100 books is in print; there are nearly 230 million copies of his books in print worldwide, making him one of the bestselling authors in modern literary history. His books have been translated into twenty languages, and more than forty-five of his novels and stories have been made into feature films and television movies.

His hardcover bestsellers include *The Lonesome Gods, The Walking Drum* (his twelfth-century historical novel) *Jubal Sackett, Last of the Breed,* and *The Haunted Mesa.* His memoir, *Education of a Wandering Man,* was a leading bestseller in 1989. Audio dramatizations and adaptations of many L'Amour stories are available on cassette tapes from Bantam Audio Publishing.

The recipient of many great honors and awards, in 1983 Louis L'Amour became the first novelist ever to be awarded the Congressional Gold Medal by the United States Congress in honor of his life's work. In 1984 he was also awarded the Medal of Freedom by President Reagan.

Louis L'Amour died on June 10, 1988. His wife, Kathy, and their two children, Beau and Angelique, carry the L'Amour tradition forward with new books written by the author during his lifetime to be published by Bantam well into the nineties.